THE
SECRET
OF
HAPPINESS

THE
SECRET
OF
HAPPINESS

I swear by God!
The sea of joy yearneth to attain
your presence, for every good thing
hath been created for you, and will,
according to the needs of the times,
be revealed unto you.

Bahá'u'lláh

The Secret of Happiness - Gift Edition

by Justice St Rain

© 2012 Special Ideas
A low-cost give-away edition can be
purchase in bulk by calling
1-800-326-1197
or visit www/interfaithresources.com

ISBN #978-1888547-27-6

The happiness of man
is in the fragrance of the
love of God.

'Abdu'l-Bahá

CONTENTS

God,

    your dearest Friend and
        the Creator of the Universe,
            wants you to be happy.

In fact,
        He wants *all* of us to be happy.

It is strange, then, isn't it,
        that so few of us *are* happy

            —*really* happy?

Happy is the soul that seeketh, in this brilliant era, heavenly teachings, and blessed is the heart which is stirred and attracted by the love of God.

— *'Abdu'l-Bahá*

O SON OF MAN!

Rejoice in the gladness of thine heart, that thou mayest be worthy to meet Me and to mirror forth My beauty.

— *Bahá'u'lláh*

There are many conflicting ideas about what makes us happy. Materialists would say that *having everything we want* will make us happy. Hedonists would say that *doing whatever we want* will make us happy. Romantics are sure that being loved by a good person will bring us happiness—which at least moves us in the direction of goodness, while religious people believe that *doing what is good* will make us happy. Since this is an inspirational booklet, you might assume that I would agree with one or the other of these last two.

But I don't.

...to love the Good and to live the Good is
the supreme thing in religion....

—William Channing Gannett

*There is but one pursuit in life which it is
in the power of all to follow, and of all to attain. It is subject to no disappointments, since
he that perseveres, makes every difficulty an
advancement, and every contest a victory; and
this is the pursuit of virtue.*

— Charles Caleb Colton

Instead of *doing* good or *being* loved, I believe that we find happiness when we, ourselves, *love* what is good and then do what we love.

How is that different from simply doing good because God wants us to?

I'll tell you.

If we don't *want* to do good, but we do "good" things anyway, then doing good becomes nothing more than a bargaining tool with which to bribe God into giving us happiness when we get to heaven. In the meantime, it will make us irritated and self-righteous, which is very different from being happy.

The one true God, exalted be His glory, hath wished nothing for Himself. The allegiance of mankind profiteth Him not, neither doth its perversity harm Him. The Bird of the Realm of Utterance voiceth continually this call: "All things have I willed for thee, and thee, too, for thine own sake."

— *Bahá'u'lláh*

We often approach God's guidance and laws as though He were giving us a list of things that we should do to make Him happy. But God doesn't need our help to be happy. God is offering to give us *His* help so that *we* can be happy. When God commands us to "...*love the Lord thy God with all thy heart, and with all thy soul, and with all thy mind...*" (MT 22:37) He is not telling us that He needs us to love Him in order for Him to be happy with us. He is telling us that we need to love what is good in the universe so that we can live happy lives.

Loving what is good is the essence of loving God. When we love what is good, then we will enjoy doing good things. This is why Faith is more important than Works.

It is recorded in the Holy Bible that God said, 'Let us make man in our image, after our likeness.' It is self-evident that the image and likeness mentioned do not apply to the form and semblance of a human being because the reality of divinity is not limited to any form or figure. Nay, rather the attributes and characteristics of God are intended. Even as God is pronounced to be just, man must likewise be just. As God is loving and kind to all men, man must likewise manifest loving-kindness to all humanity.... In a word, the 'image and likeness of God' constitute the virtues of God, and man is intended to become the recipient of the effulgences of divine attributes.

– 'Abdu'l-Bahá

Faith is a spiritual attraction to the invisible qualities of God. Works are the result of that attraction. Without the spiritual attraction, we do not enjoy doing the good works. Enjoy—that means to infuse with joy. And joy is what life is all about.

Why, in heaven's name, would loving doing good things bring us joy?

It's simple. When I talk about loving the good, I'm talking about loving the qualities, or *virtues* of God. These are the same virtues that God placed within us when He created us in His spiritual "image." These virtues include things like love, hope, faith, courage, wisdom, generosity, beauty, compassion, honesty, creativity, and so on.

Therefore, we learn that nearness to God is possible through devotion to Him, through entrance into the Kingdom and service to humanity; it is attained by unity with mankind and through loving-kindness to all; it is dependent upon investigation of truth, acquisition of praiseworthy virtues, service in the cause of universal peace and personal sanctification. In a word, nearness to God necessitates sacrifice of self, severance and the giving up of all to Him.

Nearness is likeness.

– 'Abdu'l-Bahá

When we love virtues like these, we want to surround ourselves with them. Filling our lives with people and things that reflect these qualities will certainly bring us more happiness than filling our lives with electronic games or gold. But there is more to it than that.

Each of these virtues already exists within us like tiny seeds. When we *strengthen* these virtues in our own souls, then we experience something even more powerful than happiness. It is called joy. Joy is the sensation we feel when we are moving towards God. For example, being around kind people can make us happy, but discovering and practicing our own capacity for kindness will bring us joy.

Joy is the infallible sign
of the presence of God.
— *Pierre Teilhard de Chardin*

O SON OF MAN!
Sorrow not save that thou art far from Us.
Rejoice not save that thou art drawing near
and returning unto Us. — *Bahá'u'lláh*

Any time that we respond to a situation with greater kindness, creativity, generosity or courage than usual, we feel this surge of elation. Though this intense sensation of joy may fade as we become accustomed to expressing these virtues, the underlying state of happiness, serenity and stability that comes from practicing them does not fade.

The reason for this relates to the idea of being created in the image of God. God created us to reflect His virtues in the world. It is our reason for being, and it is an expression of our true nature. Developing our virtues is simply our way of growing into the beautiful beings that God created us to become.

O SON OF BEING!

Thou art My lamp and My light is in thee. Get thou from it thy radiance and seek none other than Me. For I have created thee rich and have bountifully shed My favor upon thee.

— *Bahá'u'lláh*

True loss is for him whose days have been spent in utter ignorance of his self.

— *Bahá'u'lláh*

What we are really talking about here is becoming our true selves. *Of course* it makes us happy.

So if happiness comes from filling our lives with God's virtues, where does unhappiness come from? From the *lack* of these virtues, of course.

We feel unhappy in situations in which we need a virtue that we haven't developed yet. Every unhappiness and every difficulty can be resolved through the application of one or more virtues. For example, if we feel unhappy during financial difficulties, then the virtues of faith, hope and detachment can help us feel happier, while the virtues of perseverance, enthusiasm and will can help improve our finances.

If we are caused joy or pain by a friend, if a love prove true or false, it is the soul that is affected. If our dear ones are far from us—it is the soul that grieves, and the grief or trouble of the soul may react on the body.

Thus, when the spirit is fed with holy virtues, then is the body joyous; if the soul falls into sin, the body is in torment!

When we find truth, constancy, fidelity, and love, we are happy; but if we meet with lying, faithlessness, and deceit, we are miserable.

— 'Abdu'l-Bahá

We also feel unhappy when we think we have lost the source of a virtue in our lives. For example, the death of a loved one is a true cause of sadness.

This is a rational explanation of what makes us happy and sad but, of course, you know that we are not always rational. Our hearts operate in the world of metaphor. We have been told so many different things about how and where to find happiness that it may take a while to detach our hearts from all of the other images of happiness it has become attracted to. Fame, fortune, loves, careers—all of these things hold out the promise of happiness because they *symbolize* in the material world some inner virtue that our hearts long to experience.

O SON OF EARTH!
Wouldst thou have Me, seek none other than Me; and wouldst thou gaze upon My beauty, close thine eyes to the world and all that is therein.... — *Bahá'u'lláh*

The greatest comfort in this life is having a close relationship with God.
— *David O. McKay*

We are saddened by material losses, for example, because we mistakenly believe that possessions can bring us virtues like security or self-esteem.

But true security and self-esteem come from our relationship with God. Why allow ourselves to become distracted by the *symbol* of virtue when we can focus on discovering the *true* virtue within our own hearts?

God has given man a heart and the heart must have some attachment....

Man must attach himself to an infinite reality, so that his glory, his joy, and his progress may be infinite.

Only the spirit is real; everything else is as shadow.   — *'Abdu'l-Bahá*

God has given man a heart and the heart must have some attachment. We have proved that nothing is completely worthy of our heart's devotion save reality, for all else is destined to perish. Therefore the heart is never at rest and never finds real joy and happiness until it attaches itself to the eternal. How foolish the bird that builds its nest in a tree that may perish when it could build its nest in an ever-verdant garden of paradise.

Man must attach himself to an infinite reality, so that his glory, his joy, and his progress may be infinite. Only the spirit is real; everything else is as shadow.   — 'Abdu'l-Bahá

Attaching our hearts to the infinite world of virtue gives us control of our happiness. If we are attached to anything else, then happiness becomes unpredictable: someone is kind, someone is mean; we make some money, we lose some money. Happiness becomes an accident of fate, not the result of our conscious effort. Understanding that happiness comes from loving and developing virtues puts happiness within our control. Since the potential for every virtue is already within us, our happiness is not dependent on any outside force. No one can take it away from us.

Happiness consists not of having, but of being; not of possessing, but of enjoying. It is a warm glow of the heart at peace with itself. A martyr at the stake may have happiness that a king on his throne might envy. Man is the creator of his own happiness. It is the aroma of life, lived in harmony with high ideals. For what a man has he may be dependent upon others; what he is rests with him alone.

— David O. McKay

Think about that. You are responsible for your own happiness—not your family, friends, physical health, living environment or financial resources. This realization can be empowering, or it can overpower you with the fear of failure. In order to have confidence in your ability to be happy, you need to understand how to develop the virtues that God has given you. The first good news is that you don't have to develop them perfectly or all at once. As I said before, joy is the sensation generated by moving towards God, and even baby steps are considered movement in the realm of virtue. The second good news is that God provides us with guidance every step of the way.

...happiness does not consist in amusement. In fact, it would be strange if our end were amusement, and if we were to labor and suffer hardships all our life long merely to amuse ourselves.... The happy life is regarded as a life in conformity with virtue. It is a life which involves effort and is not spent in amusement....

— Aristotle

The Alternatives:

Some people choose to attach their hearts to the material world rather than the spiritual world. They try to spend their way to happiness or buy their way to respect, or work their way to security. But when they do these things, they fail to practice the virtues of detachment, responsibility and moderation, and actually destroy the success, security and respect that material wealth symbolizes.

People who believe that happiness is a physical sensation rather than a spiritual sensation will try to eat, drink, opiate or seduce their way to happiness. In so doing, they end up destroying the health of the very bodies whose sensations they are desperately trying to control.

But the life of man is... divine, eternal, not mortal and sensual. For him a spiritual existence and livelihood is prepared and ordained in the divine creative plan. His life is intended to be a life of spiritual enjoyment to which the animal can never attain. This enjoyment depends upon the acquisition of heavenly virtues. The sublimity of man is his attainment of the knowledge of God. The bliss of man is the acquiring of heavenly bestowals, which descend upon him in the outflow of the bounty of God. The happiness of man is in the fragrance of the love of God. This is the highest pinnacle of attainment in the human world. How preferable to the animal and its hopeless kingdom!

— 'Abdu'l-Bahá

Those who believe that happiness comes from romantic love rather than from spiritual love focus on personalities instead of virtues and become willing to compromise their values in the name of being loved. True love is a spiritual attraction towards the unique constellation of virtues that another person reflects. Anything else just leads to heartbreak.

I invite you to consider the consequences of these alternatives. These are the three paths to happiness that the majority of the world is taking, and the world is very, very sad right now.

When I invite you to develop your virtues as a path to happiness, I am not asking you to stop doing something that is currently

It is my wish that you may have at better and freer life than I have had. Recommend virtue to your children; it alone, not money, can make them happy. I speak from experience; this was what upheld me in time of misery.
— *Ludwig van Beethoven*

Virtue is its own reward, and brings with it the truest and highest pleasure....
— *John Henry Newman*

making you happy in order to try something that will be difficult and painful. I'm inviting you to stop doing the things that are already making you miserable and try something that will bring you joy from the very first moment that you try it. As I said earlier, doing good without loving good will make you miserable. But stopping the things that give you a false sense of pleasure, security or love will also make you miserable. It is only by *starting* something that brings you true joy that you will ever be able to change your patterns and live a happy life. The *something* that will bring you joy is the development of the beautiful and radiant virtues that are already in your heart just waiting to be nurtured.

People are often unreasonable and self-centered. Forgive them anyway.

If you are kind, people may accuse you of ulterior motives. Be kind anyway.

If you are honest, people may cheat you. Be honest anyway.

If you find happiness, people may be jealous. Be happy anyway.

The good you do today may be forgotten tomorrow. Do good anyway.

Give the world the best you have and it may never be enough. Give your best anyway.

For you see, in the end, it is between you and God. It was never between you and them anyway.   — Mother Teresa

How to develop virtues:

The question of how to develop virtues is almost as big a mystery in the world as happiness is. Are virtues like talent—you either have them or you don't? No. Though we are born with different innate qualities and potentials, we are each given *enough* of every virtue of God to fulfill our purpose in life. It is our job to nurture and cultivate those virtues, like tiny seeds, so that they grow and blossom, bringing joy to ourselves and the people around us. Here are some of the steps in the process.

Before we can nurture a virtue, we must be able to:

All over the world one hears beautiful sayings extolled and noble precepts admired. All men say they love what is good, and hate everything that is evil! Sincerity is to be admired, whilst lying is despicable. Faith is a virtue, and treachery is a disgrace to humanity. It is a blessed thing to gladden the hearts of men, and wrong to be the cause of pain. To be kind and merciful is right, while to hate is sinful. Justice is a noble quality and injustice an iniquity....

But all these sayings are but words and we see very few of them carried into the world of action. — 'Abdu'l-Bahá

Define it as a virtue

Recognize it in practice

Experience it for ourselves

Appreciate (or love) it

Express it in our actions

Practice it regularly

While all of these steps can conceivably take place simultaneously, it is helpful to break the steps down because each virtue may present a challenge at a different step. Our culture inaccurately defines many virtues, under-values others, expresses some very poorly, and discourages the practice of many under the false assumption that "true virtue" should come naturally without practice or conscious effort.

Happy is the man that findeth wisdom, and the man that getteth understanding. For the merchandise of it is better than the merchandise of silver, and the gain thereof than fine gold. She is more precious than rubies: and all the things thou canst desire are not to be compared unto her. Length of days is in her right hand; and in her left hand riches and honour. Her ways are ways of pleasantness, and all her paths are peace. She is a tree of life to them that lay hold upon her: and happy is every one that retaineth her.

—Proverbs 3:13-18

Defining Virtues

When Jesus said *"blessed are the peace makers,"* He was naming a virtue. When King David sang, *"Justice and judgment are the habitation of Thy throne: mercy and truth shall go before Thy face."* He was exalting virtues. And when Bahá'u'lláh, the Prophet-Founder of the Bahá'í Faith wrote, *"Be generous in prosperity, and thankful in adversity. Be worthy of the trust of thy neighbor, and look upon him with a bright and friendly face…,"* He was describing the application of virtues.

But the fruit of the Spirit is love, joy, peace, longsuffering, gentleness, goodness, faith, Meekness, temperance: against such there is no law. — *Galatians 5:22*

Whatsoever things are true, whatsoever things are honest, whatsoever things are just, whatsoever things are pure, whatsoever things are lovely, whatsoever things are of good report; if there be any virtue, and if there be any praise, think on these things.

— Philippians 4:8

Religions help us define virtues by providing us with the names and descriptions of the virtues that God wants us to develop. You will not find these virtues in your economics classes, sports commentaries, or studies of animal behavior. They do not include good looks, material wealth, or power over others.

Some virtues—like meekness and selflessness—are completely counter-intuitive and at cross-purposes with our cultural expectations. There is a reason why God's Messengers were rejected by the people of Their time. They were calling us to adopt virtues and behaviors that people really didn't want to practice—things like *turning the other cheek.*

God sent His Prophets into the world to teach and enlighten man, to explain to him the mystery of the Power of the Holy Spirit, to enable him to reflect the light, and so in his turn, to be the source of guidance to others. The Heavenly Books, the Bible, the Qur'án, and the other Holy Writings have been given by God as guides into the paths of Divine virtue, love, justice and peace.

Therefore I say unto you that ye should strive to follow the counsels of these Blessed Books, and so order your lives that ye may, following the examples set before you, become yourselves the saints of the Most High!

— 'Abdu'l-Bahá

But the virtues of God's Messengers are the virtues that our hearts were created to reflect. They are expressions of our true spiritual nature and are, therefore, the ones that will ultimately lead to our happiness.

So we learn to identify virtues by studying the Holy Writings of the world's religions. Then we have to look around us and try to recognize what they might look like in real life. It's like seeing a picture of a rose in a book, then finding one growing in a garden. The Holy Books describe virtues so that we will be better able to recognize them when we see them. But that is not enough. Some will walk through a garden, say "Yep, that's a rose alright," and go on about their lives.

The greatest gift of man is universal love—that magnet which renders existence eternal. It attracts realities and diffuses life with infinite joy. If this love penetrate the heart of man, all the forces of the universe will be realized in him, for it is a divine power which transports him to a divine station and he will make no progress until he is illumined thereby. Strive to increase the love-power of reality, to make your hearts greater centers of attraction and to create new ideals and relationships.

— *'Abdu'l-Bahá*

Recognition without appreciation is empty. This is what I meant at the beginning when I talked about loving the good. This is the key to happiness, but it cannot be forced. No one can *make* us love virtue. Appreciation of virtue, however, can be *learned*. We learn to love virtue when we get beyond fear, resistance, apathy or habit and really open ourselves up to the experience of virtue. Virtue is infinitely loveable if we just give ourselves the opportunity to experience it.

Some Lovable Virtues

Altruism
Humor
Charity
Cleanliness
Compassion
Committment
Confidence
Consideration
Contentment
Cooperation
Courage
Courtesy
Creativity
Curiosity
Determination
Devotion
Education
Empathy
Endurance
Energy

Enthusiasm
Faith
Flexibility
Focus
Forgiveness
Freedom
Friendship
Generosity
Gentleness
Grace
Gratitude
Happiness
Helpfulness
Honesty
Honor
Hope
Hospitality
Humility
Idealism
Imagination

Independence
Initiative
Integrity
Joy
Justice
Kindness
Knowledge
Love
Loyalty
Meekness
Mercy
Moderation
Modesty
Nobility
Non-Violence.
Obedience
Optimism
Patience
Peace
Perseverance
Prayerfulness
Prudence

Purity
Radiance
Resilience
Resourcefulness
Respect
Responsibility
Reverence
Sacrifice
Self-Control
Self-Discipline
Selflessness
Serenity
Service
Sincerity
Strength
Thoughtfulness
Trustworthiness
Truthfulness
Understanding
Unity
Wisdom
Wonder

Those who are not looking for happiness are the most likely to find it, because those who are searching forget that the surest way to be happy is to seek happiness for others.

— *Martin Luther King Jr.*

Everyone wants to live on top of the mountain, but all the happiness and growth occurs while you're climbing it.

— *Andy Rooney*

The Challenge of Loving Virtues

The problem with trying to cultivate virtues is that, like roses, every virtue has its thorns. The eyes and the nose may love the rose, but if you grab it by the stem, you will get hurt. Forgiveness, humility, selflessness, generosity—when people look at these virtues, they see thorns. They see the potential pain they cause in the Darwinian game of survival of the fittest. They see material inconvenience that, to them, outweighs the aesthetic charm of the velvety petals and sublime perfume. But the fragrance of the rose of virtue is the joy of friendship, kindness, serenity

May you be given life! May the rain of the Divine Mercy and the warmth of the Sun of Truth make your gardens fruitful, so that many beautiful flowers of exquisite fragrance and love may blossom in abundance. Turn your faces away from the contemplation of your own finite selves and fix your eyes upon the Everlasting Radiance; then will your souls receive in full measure the Divine Power of the Spirit and the Blessings of the Infinite Bounty.

If you thus keep yourselves in readiness, you will become to the world of humanity a burning flame, a star of guidance, and a fruitful tree, changing all its darkness and woe into light and joy by the shining of the Sun of Mercy and the infinite blessings of the Glad Tidings.

This is the meaning of the power of the Holy Spirit, which I pray may be bountifully showered upon you. — *'Abdu'l-Bahá*

and spiritual peace. These lasting joys are worth the temporary pain that we may suffer in the path of virtue.

To learn to love the rose, you must look with your eyes, not with your fist. To learn to love virtues, you must look with your heart, not your ego.

God is inviting us to experience the rose of virtue on a deeper level—to fall in love with it, to become enamored with the spiritual sensations it generates, to long for its presence in our lives. The real challenge in life is to develop such an intimate relationship with the virtues we encounter that we can't resist inviting them into our own hearts—thorns and all.

You must become distinguished for lov-ing humanity, for unity and accord, for love and justice. In brief, you must become dis-tinguished in all the virtues of the human world — for faithfulness and sincerity, for justice and fidelity, for firmness and stead-fastness, for philanthropic deeds and service to the human world, for love toward every human being, for unity and accord with all people, for removing prejudices and promot-ing international peace. Finally, you must become distinguished for heavenly illumina-tion and for acquiring the bestowals of God.
— *'Abdu'l-Bahá*

When we love virtues, we want to surround ourselves with them. It is like moving that rose into our own garden where we can nurture it, help it grow, and allow its beauty to influence the lives of the people around us. This is when we begin to want to express these virtues ourselves. It is no longer enough to admire them from the outside. We are compelled to bring them to life from within.

O FRIEND! In the garden of thy heart plant naught but the rose of love, and from the nightingale of affection and desire loosen not thy hold.
                                    — Bahá'u'lláh

I believe compassion to be one of the few things we can practice that will bring immediate and long-term happiness to our lives. I'm not talking about the short-term gratification of pleasures like sex, drugs or gambling (though I'm not knocking them), but something that will bring true and lasting happiness.

The kind that sticks.

— *Dalai Lama*

If you have ever planted a garden, you know the joy that comes from seeing a tender plant grow into a thriving source of beauty. Nurturing and expressing our virtues brings forth an even greater joy.

This is a truth that our culture really hasn't grasped yet.

The joy of expressing kindness, compassion, generosity, patience, courage or grace is not an abstract joy. It is not an intellectual joy. It is not even exclusively a spiritual joy. It is a joy that touches our hearts, our minds, and, yes, our bodies. That this truth is not universally recognized only tells us how rare the pure expression of these virtues is in the world today.

As for the spiritual perfections they are man's birthright and belong to him alone of all creation. Man is, in reality, a spiritual being, and only when he lives in the spirit is he truly happy. This spiritual longing and perception belongs to all men alike....

— *'Abdu'l-Bahá*

If we all had more experience with these virtues, we would all long for them like a starving person longs for food. And I don't mean that we would merely long to *receive* the benefits of these virtues. We would long to *express them* so that we could feel the exhilaration and ecstasy of spiritually moving towards God. When we see a rose, no one has to coerce us into inhaling the sweetness of the fragrance. Our bodies are instinctively drawn to its perfume. When we experience God's virtues within us, we naturally react the same way.

Think about that a moment.

What is inspiration?
It is the influx of the human heart.
— *'Abdu'l-Bahá*

O SON OF SPIRIT!

My first counsel is this: Possess a pure, kindly and radiant heart that thine may be a sovereignty ancient, imperishable and ever-lasting. — *Bahá'u'lláh*

Opening our Hearts to Virtue

If kindness smelled like a rose, then you could walk through a crowded room and know exactly who would make a good friend. You could enter a situation and know whether you were safe or in danger, whether a person was manipulating you or being sincerely helpful. You could use your spiritual senses to evaluate your spiritual environment the way you use your physical senses to evaluate your physical environment. Of course, first you would have to learn what a rose smelled like and experience enough roses and enough kindness so that you could recognize the scent.

When man's soul is rarified and cleansed, spiritual links are established, and from these bonds sensations felt by the heart are produced. The human heart resembleth a mirror. When this is purified human hearts are attuned and reflect one another, and thus spiritual emotions are generated.

— 'Abdu'l-Bahá

Our hearts *do* create sensations when we experience kindness. They are called emotions. *Emotions are the sensations that our hearts generate in response to the perceived presence or absence of virtues.* The problem is that we have not been taught to recognize the meaning of our emotions, nor do we have enough experience with our positive emotions to be able to associate them with the corresponding positive virtues.

Unfortunately, the same cannot be said about our negative emotions. Our hearts have lots of experience recognizing situations in which virtues are missing, needed, or actively shunned. This is why most of us have shut down our hearts and stopped listening to their message.

So great shall be the discernment of this seeker that he will discriminate between truth and falsehood even as he doth distinguish the sun from shadow. If in the uttermost corners of the East the sweet savours of God be wafted, he will assuredly recognize and inhale their fragrance, even though he be dwelling in the uttermost ends of the West.... When the channel of the human soul is cleansed of all worldly and impeding attachments, it will unfailingly perceive the breath of the Beloved across immeasurable distances....

— *Bahá'u'lláh*

In order to learn to love virtues, we must be willing to feel the pain of their absence. This is probably the most difficult part of becoming happy. We first have to come face-to-face with all of the reasons we have to be unhappy. There are so few virtues being practiced in the world today that a sensitive person may burst into tears when someone holds a door for them or gives them a compliment. Seeing virtue just reminds us of how much we long for it.

When we reach the stage where we really long for virtues, but we just aren't finding them in the world around us, that is when we turn to the Source of virtues for the light of inspiration and a shoulder to cry on.

Love is the breath of the Holy Spirit

in the heart of Man.

— *'Abdu'l-Bahá*

The state of longing for virtue—which is longing for God—is the pivotal condition. Longing for virtue—whether it leaves us sobbing at our loss or euphoric with the beauty of what is to come—has been described as the Spirit of Faith, as the Breath of the Holy Spirit, as being Born Again, as the key to Personal Transformation and as the condition of the True Seeker. God can't *make you* go there, but once you *choose* to go, He can take you anywhere.

God guides, inspires and supports us through the prayers, meditations and holy writings revealed by His Messengers. These writings are *descriptions* of God's virtues and *expressions* of them as well.

O SON OF MAN!

Veiled in My immemorial being and in the ancient eternity of My essence, I knew My love for thee; therefore I created thee, have engraved on thee Mine image and revealed to thee My beauty.

O SON OF THE WONDROUS VISION!

I have breathed within thee a breath of My own Spirit, that thou mayest be My lover.

— Bahá'u'lláh

When we are in need of support, when we need to experience virtues in our own lives, we can read the Words of God and *feel* the presence of His love and bounty right here and now.

For example, when I read *"Veiled in My immemorial being…I knew My love for thee; therefore I created thee, have engraved on thee Mine image and revealed to thee My beauty,"* my heart responds as viscerally as it does when my own father says he loves me…or perhaps more. I not only feel the love, but hope and faith rise up in my heart, assuring me that the universe *is* a kind and just place. That makes it easier for me to open my heart up to kindness and justice without fearing the pain of their absence in the material world.

Be happy and joyous because the bestowals of God are intended for you and the life of the Holy Spirit is breathing upon you
— *'Abdu'l-Bahá*

Truth is God's guidance, it is the light of the world, it is love, it is mercy. These attributes of truth are also human virtues inspired by the Holy Spirit.

— *'Abdu'l-Bahá*

Once I feel safe and secure enough to want to practice these virtues, then God provides me with plenty of guidance and advice on how to apply these abstract virtues to practical situations. Some of this guidance comes in the form of rules or laws. Don't get too scared by this. Remember, the purpose of these laws is to help us practice virtues in the material world. When we love the virtues, the laws become welcome guideposts and gentle reminders of how we want to live. If we find a particular law especially difficult to follow, it probably means that we have not discovered the beauty of the virtue it is trying to encourage.

He hath shewed thee, O man, what is good; and what doth the LORD require of thee, but to do justly, and to love mercy, and to walk humbly with thy God?

— *Micah 6:8*

Those who believe and do right: Joy is for them, and bliss (their) journey's end.

— *Islam*

God's rules often invite us to let go of a behavior that symbolizes a virtue so that we can gain the virtue itself. If we open our hearts and listen to our feelings, we will be better able to identify the virtues that we need to develop and are afraid of losing.

The Bahá'í book of laws says: "'Observe My commandments, for the love of My beauty.' Happy is the lover that hath inhaled the divine fragrance of his Best-Beloved from these words, laden with the perfume of a grace which no tongue can describe."

See how God's commandments are associated with love, beauty, fragrance, perfume and grace rather than duty, sacrifice, and obligation. God wants us to *love* the good, not simply *do* what is good.

The virtuous find joy in this world, and they find joy in the next; they find joy in both. They find joy and are glad when they see the good they have done. — *Buddhism*

Happiness is the object and design of our existence; and will be the end thereof, if we pursue the path that leads to it; and this path is virtue, uprightness, faithfulness, holiness, and keeping all the commandments of God.
— *Joseph Smith Jr.*

So if that is the case, should you ignore a law that you don't love or avoid doing good deeds that you don't enjoy? No. Though I began this booklet by saying that *doing good* without *loving good* would make you irritated and self-righteous, I will end with the advice to *practice until you achieve.* Though virtues are infinitely lovable, they take time and experience to learn to love. So it is okay to do good things even if you don't feel like it and obey laws that you don't understand. We are not being asked to jump through hoops in order to please God. We are being invited to behave in ways that will nurture qualities that are already within us.

Meditate profoundly, that the secret of things unseen may be revealed unto you, that you may inhale the sweetness of a spiritual and imperishable fragrance, and that you may acknowledge the truth that from time immemorial even unto eternity the Almighty hath tried, and will continue to try, His servants, so that light may be distinguished from darkness, truth from falsehood, right from wrong, guidance from error, happiness from misery, and roses from thorns.

— *Bahá'u'lláh*

If we follow the guidance and keep our eyes and hearts open, we are likely to discover the hidden beauty in all of God's teachings. This knowledge will make it easier to love the expression of virtues even when they feel like thorns.

If virtue promises good fortune and tranquility and happiness, certainly also the progress towards virtue is progress towards each of these things.

— Epictetus

Happiness is not a goal...it's a by-product of a life well lived.

— Eleanor Roosevelt

Are You Ready?

So the secret of happiness is to become the person God created you to be by filling both your inner and outer life with virtues. You do that by actively trying to define, recognize, and fall in love with virtues. Love comes through a willingness to ignore the thorns of inconvenience and personal hardship while striving for a deeper, more intimate experience of virtue. With love of virtues comes the desire to express and practice them in daily life. This is supported through the constant assistance of God and the Words of His Messengers.

I beg of God that thou wilt become assisted and confirmed under all circumstances to find the ease of spirit and the happiness of con- sciousness, to enter under the shadow of the Tree of Life and to perfume thy nostrils from the fragrances of the holy rose-garden....

— *'Abdu'l-Bahá*

This path to happiness is both the easiest and the most difficult that you will ever travel. It is easy because there are no secret rituals, special prayers or complicated steps to complete in order to earn the gift of happiness. There is no magic line you have to cross or anyone you need to impress. All you need to do is to love—nothing more and nothing less.

It is also the most difficult path you will ever travel, because it requires you to love—nothing more and nothing less—even in the face of difficulties.

Learning to love — what an intriguing and exciting challenge! Just thinking about it makes me ... *happy.*

O God! Refresh and gladden my spirit. Purify my heart. Illumine my powers. I lay all my affairs in Thy hand. Thou art my Guide and my Refuge. I will no longer be sorrowful and grieved; I will be a happy and joyful being. O God! I will no longer be full of anxiety, nor will I let trouble harass me. I will not dwell on the unpleasant things of life.

O God! Thou art more friend to me than I am to myself.   I dedicate myself to Thee, O Lord!

— A Bahá'í Prayer for Happiness

www.ingramcontent.com/pod-product-compliance
Lightning Source LLC
Chambersburg PA
CBHW071834020426
42331CB00007B/1723